Explorers!

Leif Eriksson

Viking Explorer

Joanne Mattern

Enslow Publishers, Inc.

40 Industrial Road   PO Box 38
Box 398   Aldershot
Berkeley Heights, NJ 07922 Hants GU12 6BP
USA   UK

http://www.enslow.com

Library of Congress Cataloging-in-Publication Data

Mattern, Joanne, 1963–
    Leif Eriksson : Viking explorer / Joanne Mattern.
      p. cm. — (Explorers!)
    Summary: Describes the life and accomplishments of Leif, son of Norseman Erik the Red, who led a group of Vikings from Greenland on a voyage which ended on the shores of North America.
    Includes bibliographical references and index.
    ISBN 0-7660-2146-7
    1. Leiv Eiriksson, d. ca. 1020—Juvenile literature. 2. Explorers—America—Biography—Juvenile literature. 3. Explorers—Scandinavia—Biography—Juvenile literature. 4. America—Discovery and exploration—Norse—Juvenile literature. 5. Vikings—Juvenile literature. [1. Ericson, Leif, d. ca. 1020. 2. Explorers. 3. America—Discovery and exploration—Norse. 4. Vikings.] I. Title. II. Explorers! (Enslow Publishers)
E105.L47M37 2004
970.01'3'092—dc22
                                2003014781

To Our Readers: We have done our best to make sure all Internet Addresses in this book were active and appropriate when we went to press. However, the author and the publisher have no control over and assume no liability for the material available on those Internet sites or on other Web sites they may link to. Any comments or suggestions can be sent by e-mail to comments@enslow.com or to the address on the back cover.

Every effort has been made to locate all copyright holders of material used in this book. If any errors or omissions have occurred, corrections will be made in future editions of this book.

Illustration Credits: © 1996–2004 ArtToday, Inc., pp. 1, 16, 20, 21, 25, 26, 31 (top), 35, 40; © 1999 Artville, LLC., pp. 4, 6 (background), 14, 32; Corel Corporation, pp. 12 (left), 17 (top), 24, 34, 42; DigitalVision, p. 43 (map); Photo by Brian Enslow, p. 15; Enslow Publishers, Inc., pp. 10; Library of Congress, pp. 6 (foreground), 9, 12 (right, top and bottom), 17 (bottom), 18, 19, 22, 28, 29, 30, 31 (bottom), 36, 37, 38, 43 (top); Painet, Inc., p. 11.

Cover Illustration: background, Monster Zero Media; inset, Courtesy of the U.S. Naval Academy Museum, painting by Edward Moran (1829–1901).

Please note: Compasses on the cover and in the book are from © 1999 Artville, LLC.

Contents

List of Maps

The Vikings explored
Iceland and Greenland.

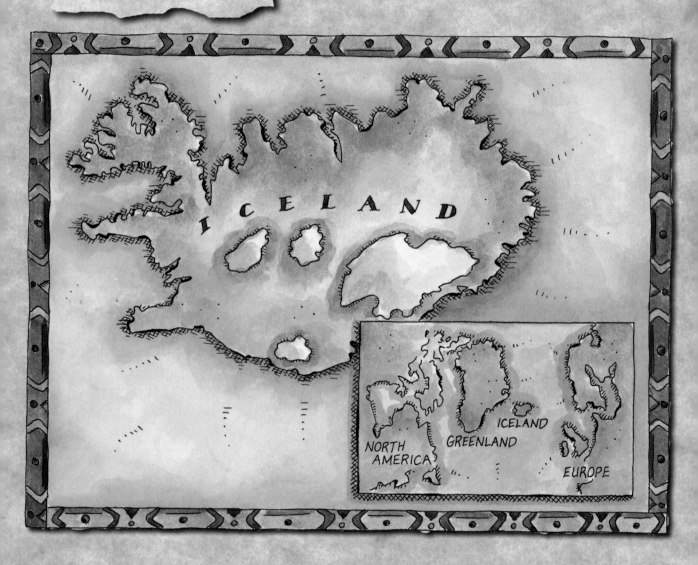

Pronunciation Guide

(Names are listed as they appear in the book.)

Leif	say "Life"
Bjarni Herjolfsson	say "Byarny Hairyolfson"
Brattahlid	say "Brattaleed"
Thjódhild	say "Teeodehild"
Thorgunna	say "Torgoona"
Thorgils	say "Torgills"
Tyrkir	say "Teerkeer"
Thorir	say "Tooreer"
Thorvald	say "Toorvald"
Skraelings	say "Skraylings"

Note: There are many spellings of Leif's last name. Some spellings are Eriksson, Eiriksson, Erikson, or Ericsson.

Leif Eriksson wanted to discover unknown lands.

Sailing West

Leif Eriksson looked over the railing of his ship. Waves slapped against the wooden longboat. Eriksson pushed his hair out of his eyes. Land should be in sight soon!

Eriksson and his crew were Vikings. They had left their homes in Greenland about a week earlier. In the year 1001, most people did not go far from their homes. But Eriksson liked discovering new things and finding new places.

A few years before, Eriksson had met a man who had sailed these waters. His name was Bjarni Herjolfsson. Herjolfsson had become lost in these waters, which were called the Western Ocean. He had seen a land that no one knew about. Herjolfsson and his men did not go ashore. Instead, they found their way home to Greenland. Herjolfsson told everyone about what he had seen. The stories filled Eriksson with excitement. He wanted to find that new land. He would go ashore and explore.

Eriksson looked to the west. There it was. He saw the shadow of land against the waves of the ocean. Eriksson yelled to his crewmen to tell them the good news.

The ship sailed toward the land. Soon it was close enough to drop anchor. Eriksson and several of his men climbed into a rowboat. They rowed to the shore. Eriksson climbed out and looked around.

The land was flat and rocky. There was no grass or trees. Behind the land, huge glaciers rose toward the sky.

Eriksson and his men did not stay on this new land very long. They rowed back to their ship and sailed away. Soon they came to other lands. These lands were covered

Leif Eriksson blew his horn. He let the crew know he had spotted the first of the three lands Herjolfsson had seen.

with trees and grass. Eriksson and his men had found a place of beauty.

Evidence of the Vikings

Eriksson and his Viking crew lived more than one thousand years ago. We know about their adventures because they were written down in a story called

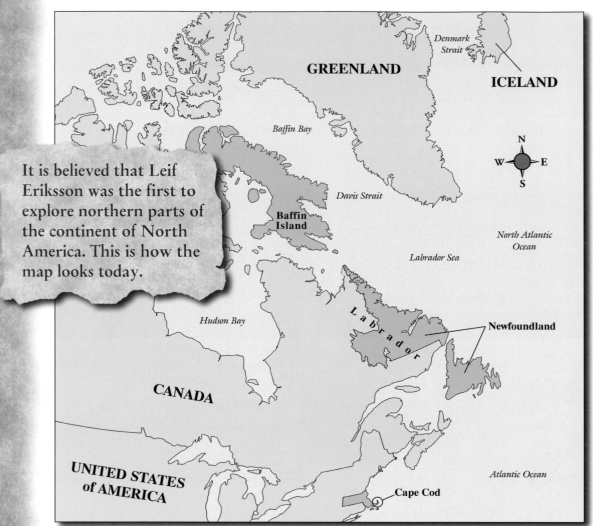

It is believed that Leif Eriksson was the first to explore northern parts of the continent of North America. This is how the map looks today.

the *Greenland Saga*. The *Greenland Saga* and other sagas tell stories about the Viking people and their lives.

Eriksson did not make a map or write down the story of his trip. The sagas were written hundreds of years after Eriksson lived. These facts made it hard to find just where Eriksson landed. Some people thought Eriksson had landed in the eastern part of Canada. Other people thought he landed near Cape Cod, Massachusetts. But no one knows for sure where Eriksson landed.

Then, during the 1960s, remains of a Viking village were found in Newfoundland, Canada. People learned more about the Vikings and about Leif Eriksson. Today, many people believe that Leif Eriksson was the first European to explore North America.

This is a replica of a Viking house in Newfoundland, Canada.

The Viking helmet was important protection during fighting.

The fierce Vikings used swords with handles like these.

Becoming a Viking

No one knows for sure when Leif Eriksson was born. He may have been born sometime around 975 in Iceland. Sometimes his name is spelled "Eriksson" or "Ericsson."

Eriksson's father was an interesting man. He was called Erik the Red. Erik got this name because of his red hair. Like his son, Erik the Red loved adventure.

Erik the Red was a Viking. The Vikings were also called Norsemen. They lived in a part of northern Europe called Scandinavia between 750 and 1100. Many Vikings sailed to other countries and attacked and robbed settlements. The Vikings were known as fierce fighters and adventurers.

Erik the Red was born in Norway. Later, he lived in Iceland for several years. One day in 980, he got into a fight with his neighbors. During the fight, Erik killed at least one man. He was called an outlaw. He was forced to leave Iceland for three years. If he stayed, anyone had the right to kill him.

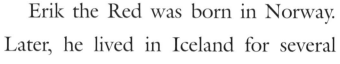

Erik the Red was a fierce Viking.

Erik had heard about land to the west of Iceland. He and some of his friends sailed west. Soon they arrived on a large island. Erik named the place Greenland. No one else lived on Greenland. Erik and his followers built a settlement there. They explored the land, farmed and fished, and made a home there.

Three years later, Erik was allowed to come home. He returned to Iceland and told people about Greenland. People liked hearing about the new land. Erik invited the Icelanders to come to Greenland.

Life was hard in Iceland at that time. There was not enough food, and the land had been overgrazed by cattle. Several hundred people said they would go with Erik. In 986,

According to legend, this is where Erik the Red left Iceland.

Viking Ships

The Vikings were very skilled shipbuilders for their time. They had a cargo ship that was used to carry goods for trade. They also had a warship, which was called the long ship. Long ships

The Vikings were very skilled sailors and shipbuilders.

were about sixty-five to ninety-five feet long. The Vikings made their ships better by adding a keel. A keel is a long, narrow piece of wood attached to the bottom of a ship. This helped the ship stay straight in the water and made it faster. Long ships had fifteen to thirty pairs of rowers and sailed well in stormy or calm weather. The prow, or front end, of a Viking long ship sometimes had a snake or dragon head carved into the wood.

twenty-five ships left Iceland and headed for Greenland. They called their home the Eastern Settlement. Erik the Red built a farm called Brattahlid, which means "steep slope." He became the leader of the Eastern Settlement.

The Skills of a Viking

Leif Eriksson grew up on his father's farm in Greenland. He lived on the farm with his mother Thjódhild, two brothers, and a sister. Greenland did not have many forests. So the settlers traded with Iceland and Norway for wood to build ships and homes. Greenland gave them animal furs, wool, and sometimes live polar bears.

Eriksson learned many things from his father and other men on the island. He learned to hunt and fish. He learned to read and write the ancient Viking symbols called runes. Eriksson also learned how to fight. Becoming a warrior was important for a Viking.

Polar bears were hunted, and their fur was traded.

Ancient Viking symbols like these were often carved into stone.

Most of all, Eriksson learned how to sail. His skill on ships impressed the people in the settlement. Once, when he was about sixteen years old, he saw a polar bear on an ice floe. Eriksson knew that if he put his boat in the water upstream from the floe, the current would carry him to the bear. Eriksson captured the bear, then used the current to bring his boat back to shore.

Eriksson was a very good hunter and sailor.

The King's Man

By the time he was a teenager, Eriksson was a very good sailor. When he was in his early twenties, Eriksson became a ship's captain for the first time. He took a crew of fourteen men with him on a trip to Norway. Most ships stopped at Iceland on the way to Norway. But the wind made Eriksson's trip last much longer than it

should have. To save time, Eriksson kept sailing and did not stop at Iceland.

Finally, the crew saw land, but it was not Norway. They were in the Hebrides, which are islands off the coast of Scotland. The same day that Eriksson and his men arrived, there was a bad storm. They could not leave the Hebrides for a month.

Eriksson was trapped for a month in the Hebrides. He waited for a terrible storm to pass.

While in the Hebrides, Eriksson stayed at the house of a local lord. He fell in love with Thorgunna, the lord's daughter. Later, she had a baby boy she named Thorgils. Eriksson was the father. When Thorgils was older, he went to Greenland to live with Eriksson.

During the next few months, Eriksson made

several trading trips. Many of these trips were to Norway. The king knew Erik the Red and was happy to meet Eriksson. He became a good friend of King Olaf of Norway.

Eriksson spent the winter of 1000 with King Olaf. During this time, he became a Christian. King Olaf was a Christian. He asked Eriksson to go back to Greenland and tell the

Eriksson became a firm believer in the Christian religion.

people about the Christian religion. Eriksson did, and many people became Christians. His mother was one of them.

When Eriksson returned to Greenland in the spring of 1000, he heard news that would change his life forever.

Herjolfsson and his men were excited to see land after a long time at sea, but it was not Greenland.

Leading a Trip

A man named Bjarni Herjolfsson said that he had found a new land. Eriksson wanted to hear Herjolfsson's story.

Bjarni Herjolfsson was a Viking sea captain from Iceland. He spent some time in Norway. When he returned to Iceland, he found his family had moved to Greenland. Herjolfsson set out to join his family, but his ship got caught in a storm.

The storm blew Herjolfsson far off course. Finally, he and his crew saw land. But this land was not Greenland. This land was covered with forests. Herjolfsson had sailed too far west and south. He turned to the north and found another land with many trees. Then he found a third land that was flat and rocky.

Herjolfsson did not want to explore these new lands. He just wanted to go home. Herjolfsson turned his ship to the east. Several days later, he finally reached Greenland and found his family.

The land Herjolfsson discovered was very different from Greenland. It was covered with trees.

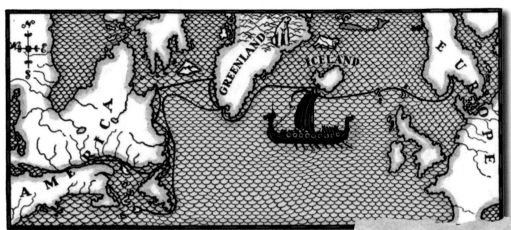

Eriksson and other Vikings sailed to Iceland and Greenland.

Herjolfsson told the Greenlanders about his trip. Many people thought he was foolish for not exploring these new places. Two of these people were Leif Eriksson and his father, Erik the Red.

Eriksson decided to explore these lands himself. Herjolfsson settled down on his father's farm and did not travel any more. He sold his boat to Eriksson. Then Eriksson found a crew of thirty-five men to go with him. These men were the best sailors in Greenland.

Eriksson knew who he wanted to lead the trip to the new lands in the west. He asked his father. Erik the Red was not sure this was a good idea. He was old.

Although Erik the Red wanted to sail one last time with his son, he knew his sailing days were over.

He thought his days of adventure were far behind him. Eriksson kept asking. Erik the Red finally agreed.

It was time for the men to leave. As Erik rode down to the dock, his horse tripped. Erik was thrown from the horse and hurt his ankle. He felt that his accident was a sign that he was not meant to go on this trip. The sagas say that Erik told his son, "I am not intended to find any other land than this one where we now live. This will be the end of our traveling together."

Eriksson's ship and crew were waiting for him. He decided to go without his father. Eriksson would lead the trip himself.

Heading West

Eriksson and his thirty-five-member crew left Greenland
in the summer of 1001. It took about a week for them
to reach one of the lands Bjarni Herjolfsson had told
them about. This new land was not much more than
a flat rock. Eriksson named it Helluland. That word
meant "Flat Stone Land." Today, some people think that
Helluland is the place we call Baffin Island. Baffin Island
is a rocky island south of the Arctic Circle. Because the
Vikings did not leave anything there, no one is sure that
Baffin Island is the place where they landed.

There was nothing to explore on Helluland, so

The first land Eriksson came across was flat and covered in rock.

Eriksson and his men got back into their ship and sailed to the south. Soon they came upon another new land. This place was very different from Helluland. It was covered with thick trees. Eriksson walked along the beach and named this land Markland, or "Wood Land." Today, people think that Markland is part of Labrador, in eastern Canada.

Although Markland looked like a beautiful place, Eriksson did not want to stay there. He knew that

While the second land was very beautiful, Eriksson was eager to find the third land.

Eriksson decided they would settle on the third land and explore.

Herjolfsson had found three lands, and he was eager to find the third place. Once again, Eriksson's ship sailed away.

Two days later, the ship landed on the third land. This land was grassy and had many trees. The *Greenland Saga* says that the men "went ashore and looked about them. The weather was fine. There was dew on the grass, and the first thing they did was get some of it on their hands and put it to their lips. It seemed the sweetest thing they had ever tasted."

Eriksson thought that this rich, beautiful land would be a good place to spend the winter. His crew towed their ship up a river and into a lake. Then Eriksson and his men built several stone huts to live in over the winter. It would be a winter of great discoveries for all of them.

Eriksson and his men spent the winter in a house like this.

These people are pretending to be Vikings in a recreated house.

Leif the Lucky

Every day, some of Eriksson's men went exploring. All of them were amazed by what they saw. There were fields full of grass. The rivers and lakes were full of large fish. Even the weather amazed them. Because they were farther south than they had been in Greenland, the sun rose earlier and set later than it did in their homeland. There was little snow or ice. This was very different from the cold weather back home.

Eriksson's men had strict orders to return to camp by nightfall. One evening, a man named Tyrkir did not come back in time. Eriksson sent some other men to

The men lived off the fish from the lakes.

find him. When they did find Tyrkir, he was very excited. He told Eriksson that he had found grapevines. Most of Eriksson's men had probably never seen grapevines, because they did not grow in Greenland. But Tyrkir had been born in Germany, so he knew what grapevines looked like.

Eriksson was excited when he saw the grapevines. Since grapes did not grow on Greenland, the Greenlanders sometimes traded for grapes with other countries. They used the grapes for food and to make wine. Because grapes were so hard to get, only rich people in Greenland could afford them. Here was a land full of the delicious fruit.

In honor of the grapes, Eriksson named this new land Vinland, which meant "Wine Land." Today, many historians think Vinland was a place called L'Anse aux Meadows in Newfoundland, Canada. Remains of Viking buildings have been found there. Some other historians think Vinland was Cape Cod, Massachusetts. They noted that grapes really do not grow as far north as Newfoundland.

The men were excited to find grapes since they were rare in Greenland.

Eriksson loaded his ship and headed back to Greenland.

Eriksson was ready to return to Greenland and tell everyone about the land he had found. When winter ended, he and his men filled the ship with grapes, vines, and wood. It was time to go home.

The weather was good for sailing, and Eriksson and his men had no problems sailing back to Greenland. They were almost there when they saw a ship stuck on a reef. The small trading ship held fifteen Norwegian men and women. Their leader, Thorir, told Eriksson that the ship had been damaged when it hit the reef.

Eriksson rescued the sailors and brought them on board his own ship. When they all arrived in Greenland, Eriksson became known as "Leif the Lucky" because of this rescue. He was given the wrecked ship's cargo as a reward. These goods, along with the wood he brought back from Vinland, made Eriksson a rich man and a hero.

The men were so grateful for being rescued that they had a celebration when they arrived in Greenland.

Leif Eriksson will be remembered for his travels to North America.

The End of the Viking Age

Soon after Eriksson arrived home in Greenland, his father, Erik the Red, died. Eriksson was now the head of the family. Eriksson became an important leader of the settlement.

Because he was the leader at home, Eriksson never returned to Vinland. He told many people about what he had seen there. Some of these people wanted to see Vinland's riches for themselves. Even though Eriksson would not travel west again, his stories got other people to follow in his footsteps. Leif Eriksson died around 1020, when he was about forty-five years old.

Tragedy in Markland

One of the people who wanted to sail to Vinland was Eriksson's brother Thorvald. In 1004, Thorvald borrowed Eriksson's ship. It had been two years since Eriksson came home with his amazing news about the grapes, vines, and wood.

Eriksson had not seen any people living in the new lands, but other explorers were not so lucky. During the winter of 1004–1005, Thorvald got into a fight with some of the people who lived in Markland. The Vikings called them Skraelings. One of the Skraelings killed Thorvald. The sagas say that Thorvald's

Many sailors followed in Eriksson's footsteps and explored Markland and Vinland.

last words were, "We have won a fine and fruitful country, but will hardly be allowed to enjoy it."

His crew buried Thorvald in Markland. They marked his grave with a cross big enough to be seen from the sea. He may have been the first European to die and be buried in North America. One year later, the men returned to Greenland without their leader.

Changing Times, Changing Settlements

Over the next fifteen years, other Viking trips arrived in Markland and Vinland. These travelers came to fish, gather grapes, and cut down wood. Then they returned to Greenland to sell their goods. The Vikings never stayed long in North America.

By 1450, about four hundred years after Eriksson's death, the Viking settlements in Greenland were gone. The weather had become colder. The winters had become harsher. People could no longer farm or raise cattle. Iceland and Norway no longer sent supplies and other goods the Greenlanders needed.

Over time, Greenland became colder.

Viking trips were long over by the 1400s, as well. By 1100, Vikings had stopped sailing and raiding settlements. They became part of communities around Europe. The Viking Age was over. It was up to the sagas now to remind people of Leif Eriksson and the Vikings.

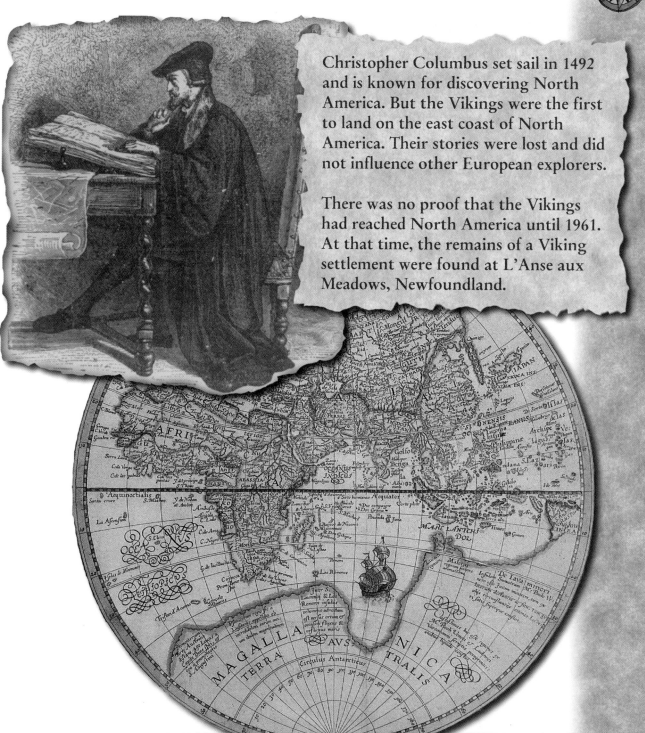

Christopher Columbus set sail in 1492 and is known for discovering North America. But the Vikings were the first to land on the east coast of North America. Their stories were lost and did not influence other European explorers.

There was no proof that the Vikings had reached North America until 1961. At that time, the remains of a Viking settlement were found at L'Anse aux Meadows, Newfoundland.

Timeline

750—The Viking Age begins.

975?—Leif Eriksson is born.

980—Erik the Red is forced to leave Iceland and sails to Greenland.

983—Erik the Red returns to Iceland to get people to join his settlement in Greenland.

986—Erik the Red brings several hundred settlers to Greenland.

1001—Leif Eriksson explores lands west of Greenland; Erik the Red dies; Eriksson becomes the leader of the Greenland settlement.

1004—Eriksson's brother Thorvald sails to Markland and Vinland.

1005—Thorvald is killed.

1020?—Eriksson dies.

1100—The Viking Age ends.

1200—The first sagas are written.

1450—There are no more Viking settlements on Greenland.

Words to Know

artifacts—Items, such as pottery or weapons, left behind by ancient people.

explore—To search for new places.

floe—A mass of floating ice.

glaciers—A large mass of ice moving slowly over an area of land.

historian—A person who studies or writes about history.

outlaw—Someone who is running away from the law.

saga—A story written in Iceland that contained history and folktales.

settlement—A small village.

Learn More About
Leif Eriksson

Books

Burgan, Michael. *Leif Ericson*. Chicago, Ill.: Heinemann Library, 2002.

Carter, W. Hodding. *An Illustrated Viking Voyage: Retracing Leif Eriksson's Journey in an Authentic Viking Knarr*. New York: Pocket Books, 2000.

Klingel, Cynthia Fitterer, and Robert B. Noyed. *Leif Eriksson: Norwegian Explorer*. Chanhassen, Minn.: The Child's World, Inc., 2002.

Langley, Andrew. *You Wouldn't Want to Be a Viking Explorer!: Voyages You'd Rather Not Make*. Danbury, Conn.: Franklin Watts, 2001.

Margeson, Susan M. *The Viking*. New York: Dorling Kindersley Publishing, Inc., 2000.

Wright, Rachel, ed. *The Viking News*. Cambridge, Mass.: Candlewick Press, 2001.

Learn More About
Leif Eriksson

Internet Addresses

Eric the Red: Explorer

<http://www.enchantedlearning.com/explorers/page/e/ericthered.shtml>

Read more about Leif Eriksson's father, Erik the Red.

Leif Ericson

<www.mnc.net/norway/Leif.htm>

This site offers a list of links to Leif Eriksson Web sites.

The Vikings

<http://www.bbc.co.uk/schools/vikings/index.shtml>

Learn more about the Vikings and their life.

Index